ONCE ONLY

Preface

jonivan is a life force, finding no barriers that cannot be moved aside in his exciting journey through life.

We are friends, bonded together by the realization of the tremendous potential that lies within each human soul. For seven years the tides of our lives have moved in and out of many human beings and many aspects of our society; jonivan leaving a distant remembrance of a unique individual.

This, his first book, is the beginning of his sharing—rooted in the importance of being yourself.

jonivan finds words as building bridges of understanding, creating feelings of comfort and inner peace.

Walter Rinder

ONCE ONLY

A collection of poems by

jonivan

Edited and illustrated by SandPiper Studios

Blue Mountain Press ™

Boulder, Colorado

Printed in the United States of America

Library of Congress Number: 78-75370
ISBN: 0-88396-044-3

First Printing: March, 1979
Second Printing: February, 1980

Acknowledgments: Thanks to the SandPiper Studios staff, including
Faith Hamilton, Cliff Scott, Craig Francis and Douglas Pagels.

Blue Mountain Press INC.

P.O. Box 4549, Boulder, Colorado 80306

Dedication:
To Walter Rinder, Lowell, Esta and Family, Bud, Stacey
To many a brother
To many a sister
and countless inspirations.

Introduction

Once Only

Let life as it reaches out to you, give you all the new experiences made easier by the old experiences of the past. Do not forget who you are, to become another person's wish, dream or desire.

Be who you are, and cry if you must, openly.

Allow no one to rob you of the personal touch you learned to activate your feelings and decisions.

Only play the games you learned were your games, and get out of those whose rules do not apply to you. You cannot lose with yourself.

No one has the rights or wrongs of making you happy for the rest of your life. Your life will only be happy if you first fulfill your own needs, instilling your own happiness, even when others would have you unhappy or alone.

There are no reasons you should ever have to be alone, so don't be. You don't have the time.

Do not look upon people's faces and hold yourself responsible because they are not smiling.

Let your smile recognize them as parts of your being, but remain your own reflection.

Let yourself find peace with the beginning of every new adventure.

Again and again, and again, grow.

Life is Once Only.

 jonivan

Reach out
 in the early morning mist,
As the day's sun
Breaks the calmness of night,
And rise to the new day,
A new awareness of being.

Shake hands with the world
And smile.

It's great to be alive.

I want to be a part of your world
having you become a part of mine.
Though we don't see eye to eye
on all that surrounds us —
our ideals in life,
our motives for being,
our reasons for existence,
I want to understand you —
even greater
accept you as you are —
with an open eye,
an open heart —
I want
to be your friend.

Time is of love
understanding is of care
patience is of virtue
needing is of wanting
desires are of dreams
hopes are of prayers
in all of these
is something
I love.

You.

I awaited your coming
so
we could exist together

You and I.

So
we could be aware
of all the todays
and find dreams

in all the tomorrows.

One unity
a togetherness
a binding strength of two
a mutual bond
a newness
an awareness of being.

A combination
of one with one
linked
joined
weaved in
and about the other.

It becomes
a you and I world.

If I give you this heart now
  someday you may never seek another

If I give you my touch
  someday the feeling will be near

If I give you my Love now
  tomorrow will find it loving

If I give you me
  someday you may give me you

If I give you my body now
  someday you'll search my soul

But if I wait until tomorrow
  to give you these things

    Tomorrow may never come.

17

Become You

If you do not think about living
life will pass you up
If you hide from adventures
your growth will diminish

If you fear new experiences
your knowledge is secondhand
If you turn love away
it finds hours of making you alone

If you do not touch
with your hands
your heart
those that are around you
may become strangers

If you do not see beauty in people
then the life you live
will find discolor

If you cannot listen to words
that are spoken
you will miss the dreams of living

So become what you are –
the inner soul of humanity
Become yourself

Touch everything
knowing it has outline
boundary

See all your eyes can see
light, beauty and sorrow

Listen
for all words
need ears to fall on

Time will show you
if you do not think about living
life will pass you up

So become
what you are

Become you.

All I need are questions to be answered
All I want is sincerity
All I take is what I give in return
All I look for are adventures to living
All I ask for is the opportunity to share
All I know is that I try to learn
All I think is what I'll experience
All I see is a beginning to each day
All I touch is reaching back
All I feel is want for love
All I accept is what is here
All I give is my energy
All I find are new paths to follow . . .

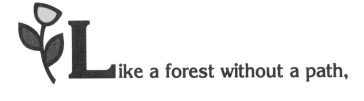 **L**ike a forest without a path,

to love without understanding
is to be lost.

Take my hand.

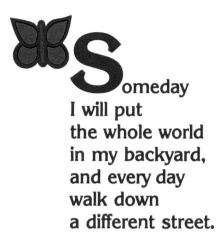

Someday
I will put
the whole world
in my backyard,
and every day
walk down
a different street.

I found myself walking this morning
down a path seeming to be walked
by many before me.
It was laden with flowers,
towering trees
and sounds that rang in the air.

I reached out to take it in
and brought to me
the richness of the morning breeze,
the feelings of warmth
through my fingertips,
life through my lungs,
love through my soul.

I came alive with humanity,
with man,
with body,
with mind.

We so often look for reasons,
forgetting we are reason.

We so often look for purpose,
forgetting we are purpose.

We so often look for Love,
forgetting we are Love.

Forgetting
we are human.

The movements of muscles
the drifting words of thoughts
the hours of wondering . . .
all put together
make what is human.

If you were to create my Loves
or build my attitudes
you must afford the time
it takes to understand
what Loves are needed
to create a man.

Man is but the grace of a thousand years,
the beginning of eternity.
Man is but the stream that grows
to be a river at journey's end.
Man is but a tree finding his way,
his destined path towards the greatness
that is heaven.
Man is but flesh and blood,
needing to be taught love and understanding.
Man is but the child of time,
learning with the decades and eons of eternity.
Man is man, no matter how small
or big he feels.
He is the symbol of a complex life
in a simple world.

If you ask me
where I have been,
I will tell you
    "In my own world,
    for none other has
    existed"

If you ask me
where I am now,
I will tell you
    "On the threshold
    of a dream
    that will change
    my life"

If you ask me
where I am headed,
I will tell you
   "One must be
     a good follower
     before one
     can become
     a good leader"

If you ask me
where I can go,
I will tell you
   "With new ways
     and new places,
     having you beside me –

   I can go anywhere"

Someday

I will walk with you,
adventuring life together

I will talk with you,
growing through experiences

I will listen with you,
finding truth in words

I will sleep with you,
knowing touch
as being part of Love

I will understand you,
hoping you understand me

I will awake with you,
knowing a new day
    a better way
Thus learning . . .
    a new love

omeday my friend
we
will know Love –
of its existence
In time –
existing within it
becoming part of it

You and I.

As our time together
is not really known
by either of us
let us
   while together
experience
   what togetherness is.

For it is when
   tomorrow becomes
the shadow of yesterday
that we may
   only then
realize that while
this day was in the passing
we were
   giving.

Let me feel my body
   it will make me more
   at ease with yours
Let me think my thoughts
   so as I speak
   you will know those things
   that are true to me
   for me
Let me be who I am
   so that I can be me
Let me give what I can
   in such a way
   that you will receive
   what I give freely
   so I will not wear out
   my usefulness in giving
Let me experience now what I feel
   in all these things
   so we can grow
   from my learning
   how to be with
   others such as us . . .

There is no love greater
than that which
gives a man a smile . . .

rather than taking it away.

How can we forget
the things
that make us
smile
in each other's arms?

It was in the winter
that rains fell
making walks along soggy paths
warm in each other's grasp

It was in the spring
flowers found time to bloom
and hearts yearned for new feelings

It was in the summer
thoughts played
among minds of men
making them children
of living

It was in the fall
hearts grew fond
the winter dreams appeared
for the recycle
of a new beginning
together

I am here for you
I am here for me
I have come
for the both of us.

We have a long way
to go
just to the beginning . . .

Longer yet, I hope
to the end . . .

together.

I have searched long for the peace
    I found with the nearness of your being
I have touched many lives in my journey
    to understanding
    my brothers and sisters better
I have listened with open ears
    finding truths evident
    among many spoken words
I have felt the longing to be one with you
    a beginning to a new acceptance
    through our message in sharing
I have given energy
    in less degrees than my worth
    sowing only what I hope
    to reap someday

Most important . . .

I have loved you
　　beyond that which you could accept
　　readily without hesitation

My God is known
My soul is young and needing
My being is existing
My heart is wanting

May this love not fear
　　those whom it finds needing
May my touch bring
　　new awareness to living
May I offer new understanding
　　through new experiences
May I share in thoughts, in new ways
　　for lives I'll never know
　　the one feeling man most needs . . .

The word God called Love

The littleness of my being
is the greatness of my love

Be at peace
with these thoughts

And know I love you
as I love myself

My love
is as it should be . . .

yours and mine.

The moments that were you
the moments that were me
The days and hours that passed
when we didn't know
each other existed
Though we had been together
we had been apart

We had yet to learn to love
the love that makes
moments
hours
and days
pass together

The love I've learned with you

A gentle drift of words –
a myth of today
a dream of tomorrow
a whisper of understanding;
of acceptance
of childish thoughts
of playing it together
of adult desires
of working it together

The gentle drift of love
our way.

Do not neglect your youthfulness
Live it slowly
Touch it earnestly
Need it carefully

It is often shattered by those
who will make you grow up
in order to be "grown up"

In the early stages
of our growth,
When in the shadows
of learning,
We find we
are alone . . .
We find warmth
in the parts
we want to play.

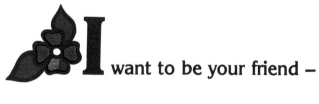I want to be your friend –

someone to talk to,
someone to relate to,
someone to listen to.
I want to find
a link of mutual understanding
whether different in personality
or extreme in character,
whether self-discipline allows
acceptance of actions
or tolerance
of individuality.

Looking up through
the massing
of stars . . .
I realized
   there was no star
   the same star
as the star you are.

May each tomorrow
remind you of yesterday
in a small way,
and may I cross the path
of your dreams
and thoughts occasionally,
looking for a
new place to ponder
in your moments
of solitude.

When one dreams freedom,
it is discovered through illusions.

When one needs freedom,
it is discovered through wants.

When one feels freedom,
it is discovered through doing.

Reach out . . .
Freedom
is just to touch
what lies at fingertip's edge.

I do not know enough
that I cannot be taught more

I do not love enough
that I cannot love more

I do not feel enough
that I cannot touch more

If we fear
new experiences,
our knowledge
is secondhand.

The course of human nature
does not guarantee us
that we will always
be together –

Only that
once we have met,
we will always
know of each other

O nce
because I touched you,
I learned what you were about.
Once
I learned of your moods,
your silhouetted feelings,
your heart's desires.
Once
I experienced your needs
to be loved,
to be wanted
to be found.
Once
I felt you as a part of me.
So I touched you again.

If only the day
and the hour would
stop
And the whole world
along with time,
so I could in my imagination
hold you there in that moment
which would touch me most.

Being with you.

I wish I could stop dreams,
Pull them out,
Shape them in front of me.
If this feat I could accomplish,
You would be here,
Instead of there.

Look
to the future
and not to the past
to find
those things
you
want to
make last

I do not want
to make reasons
for you to stay,

Only reasons
for you
to return.

jonivan

I hear the name
and see the face,
but what does it mean
and from where does he stem?
It is a name of earth
and trees and all that grows.
Of wind and rain
and gentle breezes
in the night.
And the face of a fawn,
peaceful and content.
I know him not,
but I know him well.

—Tab J.